The Universal Law Of Attraction

Crea

By N... Roberts

"I am tomorrow, or some future day, what I establish today. I am today what I established yesterday or some previous day."

~James Joyce~

ISBN: 9781520724676

The author of this book does not dispense medical advice or prescribe the use of any technique as a form of treatment for physical, emotional, or medical problems without the advice of a physician, either directly or indirectly. The intent of the author is only to offer information of a general nature to help you in your quest for emotional and spiritual well-being. In the event you use any of the information in this book for yourself, which is your constitutional right, the author and the publisher assume no responsibility for your actions.

For Pepper

My Guardian Angel, forever in my heart.

Table of Contents

Preface - Law Of Attraction Changed My Life

"I am tomorrow, or some future day, what
I establish today. I am today what I established
yesterday or some previous day"

~ James Joyce~

This quotation holds very deep meaning for me. Looking back, I can clearly see the Law of Attraction working in my life, but unfortunately not in the way I wanted. Now I know better, I have come to understand and apply one of the most amazing Laws of the Universe, The Law of Attraction. It has truly changed my life unimaginably for the better.

Before I had this knowledge I was a lost soul. Born into a dysfunctional family I suffered a childhood of confusion, violence, fear and trauma. I went on to relive those same patterns in adulthood, often ending up in violent or tumultuous relationships, completely unaware I had the power to change this at any time.

I was a living breathing example of Law of Attraction ***not*** being utilised for the good. By wallowing in my 'reality' and stumbling from one disaster to another I was telling the Universe continuously that ***this was*** my reality. I was reinforcing it by believing that *'this was all I was good for'* that *'this was all I deserved'*. It was at 35 years old and 3 suicide attempts later before I discovered something that was to change my life so beautifully and completely that I am today a happier, healthier more abundant version of myself and all because I found out about The Law of Attraction and how to utilise it for the good.

The first time I was actually aware of the forces of The Law of Attraction in my life was in 2007. I was in a very dark place indeed. I had split up from my husband, was a single mother, bankrupt, seriously depressed from traumatic events that had happened in my life and felt trapped. I was desperate for a holiday to break the cycle of misery - but didn't have the money to go.

I didn't realise that the more I focused on all of the negative things in my life, the more I was perpetuating them. In absolute despair I cried out loud 'Please, if there really is anyone or anything out there, show me what to do!'

Within a day of this plea I unexpectedly received a phone call from an agent in London who wanted to make a documentary about my life experiences in Africa (I had lived there for 5 years). I was paid a fee and it was exactly what I needed to break the monotonous cycle that my life had become. With the money I was able to take a luxury holiday with a friend and finally get a break but best of all, during the filming of the documentary I met a woman called Mfanwe who was to change my life forever.

It was during the after filming party that I told her how I had made a desperate plea from the heart and all of a sudden things had started to change for the better. She asked me if I had watched a film called 'The Secret' I told her that I hadn't and she immediately recommended that I should. She said that it would change my life beyond belief. And it did!

By changing the way in which I thought and learning to harness the Law of Attraction, my life started to change for the better, hour by hour, day by day. I learned that instead of focusing on how bad things were, to instead focus on all of the things that were good in my life. My daughter, my cats, the fact that I had a roof over my head, food in the fridge and good friends. Within a year things started to take a dramatic turn for the better and everyday as I learn more and more about the power of the Universe and put it into action in my life I see the wonderful results.

To date I have manifested a lovely home full of beautiful things, multiple holidays around the world, better health, bills paid and a solid knowledge that no matter what, things always work out. The last might have been the biggest gift of all, because it enables me to stop worrying about the future which in turn brings me into better alignment with source energy, which in turn brings me more of that which I want.

I decided to write this Book in order to share this wonderful gift of knowledge that can change your life for the better too.

Introduction - Law Of Attraction-The Basics

"The greatest discovery of my generation

is that human beings can alter their lives by

altering their attitudes of mind"

~ William James~

For those of you who have never heard about the Law of Attraction, here is a brief explanation of how it is working in your life right now. It was through watching a film called 'The Secret' that I started to understand The Law of Attraction and would recommend everyone who is new to The Law of Attraction to watch it.

I would like to start by asking you a question? What do you suppose attracted you to this book? Was it the title that got your attention? Or perhaps you were gifted it? Either way I have learned that there are very few coincidences in this world. Things normally happen for a reason.

Your life is supposed to feel good and no matter your current status, it can always get better. You have a right to happiness, abundance and prosperity. This book will explain and offer you tools for how you can reach your full potential and live the life you have always dreamed about.

The Science Behind The Law of Attraction

The truth is you and everyone else around you, in fact ***everything*** is made up of energy. You are made up of the same stuff that is in each and everything around you including the Sun, the Stars and of course even planet Earth. You are made up of cells which in turn is made up of atoms which is made up from subatomic particles and subatomic particles are of course - energy!

We are all connected to a greater whole even though most of us don't realise it. We are part of a greater power. The power of the universe and everything in it. Some call it source energy, some call it God. It doesn't matter what you call it but only to know it exists. That power and wisdom is ours for the taking if only we are able to harness it.

All of our energy is linked in much the same way that the Internet exists. You cannot see it with your five senses, yet you know that it exists and it also works to connect us together otherwise you wouldn't have been able to buy and read this book today!

I don't know if you have ever watched those science programs on the TV that wire up an athlete to a brain monitor? They have proven that when the athlete visualizes the race that he is going to run and runs it in his mind, the same receptors in his brain fire exactly as they would if he was actually running the race. Basically, the mind doesn't know the difference between actually running the race or imagining the race. How powerful is that! This demonstrates that thoughts can seriously affect us in a physiological way. If we watch a horror movie our hearts beat faster, blood pressure can rise, hands might sweat. Our brain does not always distinguish between fact and fiction. Every single cell in our bodies react to our thoughts. This is why we need to be so very careful of what we think about.

Because of our universal connection, our thoughts and emotions become like magnets - we attract what we are thinking about. Negative thoughts attracts negative things and positive thoughts attract positive things. Although it goes even further than that. Can you remember a time when you have been thinking of someone with fondness and thinking how very long it has been since you have seen or spoken to them, when all of a sudden, the phone rings or the doorbell rings and there they are, at the door or on the end of the phone? Well that is the Law of Attraction working at its best. Our thoughts travel through space at a stupendous pace and whether we have picked up on their intention to call us or our thoughts have stimulated them to call us, the result is the same.

Scientific breakthrough in Quantum Physics has been able to prove that by simply observing something we can actually change the outcome! Imagine how powerful that makes you.

Be Careful What You Wish For!

You are more capable of changing your life than you could possibly imagine and your thoughts are like a magnet, constantly attracting people and things into your life that consciously or subconsciously you have thought about. Some of these things in the past may not have been good. The thing is, The Law Of Attraction doesn't differentiate between good and bad, it just obeys. It is like the law of gravity, it doesn't care if you are falling from a 20 floor building or just jumping up and down, the result will be the same - you will come back down to earth. So it is wise to start to consciously monitor our thoughts and change the negative into positive.

I will give you an example - You may have some debt that is really worrying you and you decide to ask the Universe to help your situation, but if you are asking in a way that is filled with hopelessness, despair and you are thinking about debt, debt and more debt, what are you going to attract? That's right, debt. Because the universe only obeys the thought that you are sending out and the emotion that is accompanying it. Instead you should be thinking of abundance, abundance, abundance and feeling joy.

Visualization is a very important tool and will be discussed more later, but in this case you should be visualizing yourself paying your bills easily, cheques dropping in your mail box, money appearing in your bank account. Feel happiness as you visualize this because the emotion behind the thought is very important in the process. Good emotions raise your vibration and not only will you feel better within yourself, but you will have started on the road to changing the way that you deal with negative things in your life and will have set in motion very powerful forces that will change things for the better.

But Why Doesn't The Law Of Attraction Work For Me?

Destiny is not a matter of chance, it is a matter of choice; it is not a thing to be waited for, it is a thing to be achieved.

~William Jennings Bryan~

I cannot tell you how many times I have heard or read this on-line. Some people find out about the Law of Attraction and only understand it on a very superficial level. They misunderstand the Law of Attraction to be some magical tool and if they wish hard enough surely whatever they want will manifest. When this doesn't immediately happen they get disheartened and discard the Law of Attraction as rubbish. Maybe you are one of those people? If you are, I have good news for you. Not only does the Law of Attraction work, it is working in your life ***right now as you read this book!***

A good analogy mentioned previously is gravity. Do you think gravity is magic? Of course not. Most people correctly believe it to be a scientifically understood process. The Law of Attraction is exactly the same. It's not somemumbo jumbo magical process but instead a scientific law that operate in everyone's lives all the time whether they believe it or not. The same as gravity.

So the question is not ***whether*** it works - but ***how*** to make it work for me?

Well, the answer is more than just asking for what you want and hoping for the best. It is a matter of life choices. It requires a commitment on your part. It's a life style. As Abraham Hicks so beautifully put it, it's about ***following your bliss***. Your emotions are your compass telling you whether you are on the right track or not. Simply put, whilst you are feeling good you are attracting great things into your life. Another word commonly used for this is 'allowing', but if you are feeling negative emotions (resistance) you are generally attracting more negative things into your life.

So the choices you make in your life, i.e. to choose whether to allow positive and good feeling thoughts versus negative and bad feeling thoughts and following up on that by doing what makes you feel happy 'following your bliss', is the difference between failure or success in harnessing the Law of Attraction. Even negative experiences can have a positive spin put on them by understanding that they create contrast. If you know what you ***don't want***, it creates contrast which shows you what you ***do want*** and by following and focusing on the solution rather than the problem, you can turn things around immediately.

Tools such as Dream Boards and Wish lists, Affirmations and Visualisation all have their place in helping you to hone your skills and create your reality the way you want it to be, but at the end of the day, it's your emotions that give you the indicator as to whether you are on the right path or not. You are the creator of your own destiny, make sure you are creating your hearts desires!

"Welcome to Planet Earth. There is nothing that you cannot be, or do, or have. You are a magnificent creator."

~Abraham Hicks~

The Importance Of Thoughts And Emotions

"It is only with the heart that one can see

rightly, what is essential is invisible to the eye."

~Antoine de Saint-Exupéry~

Do you know that your feelings and emotions create a vibration and are actually more powerful than your thoughts alone? Whilst it's true that the two are connected, i.e. you could be thinking I am in debt and feeling hopeless, you could equally be thinking - 'I want to be abundant,' but instead feeling very hard done by. It is the ***emotion*** that creates the vibration which is being recognized by the Universe. This is why it's very important that you program your mind with the thoughts that you choose and make sure that your feelings and emotions match the thoughts, so that you are sending out the right vibration to the Universe.

Obviously if you are thinking about sad, worrying or depressing thoughts, you are sending out those emotions. Sad, depressed and worried. The Universe will then oblige by sending you more of the same. Remember that your vibrations are like a magnet and The Law of Attraction does not distinguish between good or bad vibrations, it only obeys and return you more of the same. So it's absolutely essential that you monitor your thoughts and change your thinking patterns.

You may think that this is not as easy as it sounds and you are right. To someone who is going through heartache, illness or stress it is very hard to break the habit of a lifetime and start to consciously change their thoughts. The chapter about Gratitude can really help with this, because if you are counting your blessings it automatically lifts your vibration, the result is going to be that you are putting out positive vibrations that will in turn start to bring you a brighter happier future.

Don't forget you can change your life ***right here right now***. It's never too late to start. The minute you change your thinking habits and start to project all of the good emotions - happiness, gratitude, joy, love and peace things ***will*** start to change for the better. Things will have been set in motion that if followed through will bring you what you wish for. Obviously things won't immediately, this very second, manifest themselves i.e. a ton of money just appear in front of your eyes, but you will have planted a seed that with the right nurturing will develop into a real and tangible change in your life.

There has been many occasions when I have needed extra money for an unexpected bill and after asking the Universe for the money, (be precise about what you want) visualising it, sending out joy and thanking the Universe as if I have already received it, I got the money that I needed before the date that I needed it. It may have come via a gift, extra work came up suddenly or any other means, but I have always received it!

When asking the Universe for things, ***don't worry about how you will get it***, don't try and visualise the way in which you might get it because you will be limiting yourself to the ways in which it could arrive. Instead, open your mind and just let it happen. Watch out for signs, depending on what the request is (money, meeting a life partner or anything else) keep your mind open to any opportunities that may come your way that could lead to your wish coming true. The Law of Attraction always works but it works in its own way - not necessarily in a way you might expect. But always remember, thoughts are a great tool to change your feelings and emotions, but your emotions and feelings are what really send out that all important vibration that will change your life for the better.

The Power Of Gratitude

"A moment of gratitude makes a difference in your attitude"

~ Bruce Wilkinson~

Never underestimate the power of gratitude! When writing about the Law of Attraction you will always have one or two people reading it who feel that things are so bad for them right now that they are going to find it nearly impossible to ever get a positive mindset. Indeed they don't really have any idea where to begin. I understand this because I myself have been there.

Looking back to when things were really bad - before I had fully understood how to utilise this amazing gift to my benefit - I too was at a loss as to how I could ever get my mind in alignment with positive thinking when everything around me was so bad. Creditors were harassing me, I was a single mother with very little family support, I had a lot of health issues and was severely depressed, but I read something that really helped me make a start and that is what I want to pass on to you today. ***The amazing power of gratitude.***

Even though things may seem really impossible for you right now, the way in which to change this and your mind set, is to stop for a moment and really think about everything in your life that is good. It may not be much or it may be a lot, depending on your circumstances, but focus on those things that are positive or good.

For me it was my wonderful daughter who is healthy and happy, my sweet little cats, the fact that I had food in the fridge and a decent roof over my head. In fact I realised that compared to some people I had so much to be thankful for that my heart filled with joy and for the first time I started to feel that dark cloud lifting from my heart and mind.

For you it could be that you have your health, a great job, wonderful friends and family or simply that you are alive. You only to have to look at people living on the street with nothing, no roof over their head, health in tatters, begging for food etc to really put things in perspective!

So how to do it? Well the first thing of course is to think of all the things that are good in your life. Let your mind caress your thoughts, enjoy the good feeling that you get when you think about something or someone important in your life. Send that happiness and gratitude out into the universe and just watch how the universe will respond by bringing you more and more things and people to be grateful for. Because positive is like a magnet for things positive and the more that you send out those wonderful vibrations the more the universe will respond by sending you more of the same. Not only that, but you will feel far better within yourself for doing so.

I normally suggest to people that the best way to start is to list all of the things you are grateful for first thing in the morning and the last thing at night. This will get you into a routine and it will soon become a natural process. But of course, also feel free to do it whenever you feel the urge. If you happen to look out of the window and see something beautiful (maybe a sunset or sunrise) let that wonderful feeling wash over you and uplift you and send out thanks into the universe for such uplifting and wonderful things. If someone gives you a unexpected gift or a kind word send out your gratitude for this. Once you are living in a place of gratitude you will find that it comes so naturally that you scarcely have to think about it.

Some people use an object to remind themselves to stop for that moment in their lives and to send out their thanks. They use anything from a piece of jewellery to a pretty stone or crystal but to be honest it could be anything strategically placed to remind you to send out a little joy and thanks. You could place your object next to the kettle or coffee machine so you will be reminded first thing in the morning or maybe in your pocket so every time you put your hand there you will be reminded! Writing things you are grateful for in your journal is also a powerful tool. Just watch how things will change in your life as a result.

Do you remember how I mentioned in an earlier chapter how thoughts effect your physical body? Well some people who practise daily gratitude find that it actually helps them with their ailments. It can help insomnia because it relaxes your mind to feel happiness and joy. It can also help with depression and all kinds of stress related illnesses, aches and pains. Just watch as you start to feel better and attract more and more wonderful things using The Law of Attraction.

Don't try to force it though, remember it is the emotion that carries the power. It won't work if you just coldly list things in your head and then go on your way. You have to actually ***feel*** the accompanying emotion of joy and happiness because ***that*** is what sends out that all important vibration that in turn attracts back more of the same.

Visualisation - A Powerful Tool

"Create a vision of who you want to be,

and then live into that picture as if it were already true" ~ Arnold Schwarzenegger~

I have already mentioned in a previous chapter about how your emotions are very powerful. It is these emotions that send out those strong vibrations that in turn attract whatever your emotion is back to you. But it goes much further than that - Visualisation can help you to pinpoint exactly what it is that you are trying to attract into your life and what's more, visualising helps you to direct that emotion far more powerfully into the Universe.

Just for a moment, as you read this, stop and ask yourself, what is it ***right now*** that you really want to attract into your life using The Law of Attraction? It might be something quite small, like a cup of tea or coffee. Or it may be something life changing - like a life partner or financial security. It could be your dream house or maybe your dream car. Whatever it is, doesn't it make you feel happy just thinking about it?

Let's use a house as an example. Maybe you have been inside it already or maybe you just have a picture, either way use your imagination to see that house as if you were already living in it. See yourself walking about the gardens and the pleasure you would feel knowing that you are the owner of this house. If you know how the inside looks imagine yourself living in that house, how you would feel waking up in the morning and looking around your new bedroom. Cooking in the kitchen and all of the things that you would like to do in that house. Immerse yourself in the joy of living in this house.

It is very important that when you visualise - you feel ownership, as if it's already yours, because that is the key to attracting things into your life. When doing this the seed will have been sown and as you visualise this day by day the Universe will have already set in motion things that will eventually lead to your dream coming true. I cannot stress enough that the most important thing is belief, because if deep down you really don't believe that this will happen, it most probably won't.

Belief and positivity are the key ingredients that will help you achieve your dream. The more positive you are about your dream and the more powerful the emotion you feel when visualising it, the faster it will be attracted into your life. A word of warning though. When visualise you must be vigilant to not feel the lack of it, otherwise that is what you will attract, lack!

Shhhhhh I'll Tell You A Secret

There is something great that I want to share with you that really surprised and pleased me when I first found out about the Law Of Attraction - Guess what? The universe doesn't know the difference between you visualising a mansion or a shed or £1 or £1,000,000! It is only our own 'self limiting beliefs' that stop us getting the larger amount. If we believe it to be beyond our reach then the Universe will oblige and it shall be so.

Whereas most of us can imagine getting £1 or even £1000 most of us would find it difficult to believe that we could really have £1,000,000. But that is our own limitation. The Universe knows nothing about it, it will only bring you what you believe is possible. This is why I always advise people to start with (what they perceive to be)small things that they believe wholeheartedly is possible and then, as they start to see these smaller things manifest in their lives, they can move onto (what they perceive to be) larger things as their confidence grows! The next chapter explains how a vision board or dream board can help with this.

One thing to remember is that it's not always about achieving the end result (although that is very nice). Don't put your life on hold whilst you wait for your dreams and desires to come true. Our desires will always grow and change, you never get it done. Once you have reached one goal you will wish for another. This is the nature of life and the Universe. The journey should be every bit as joyous as the end goal. That's the trick to successful manifesting. It should feel natural, fun and never like a chore!

Visualisation - Create A Dream/Vision Board

"Just put forth a clear enough request and

everything your heart desires must come to you."

~Mahatma Gandhi ~

I want to share with you how to make and use a vision board. It has been an incredible help to me and I have watched in amazement as thing after thing on my board has become reality!

When visualising, the subconscious mind cannot really distinguish between an imagined thought or an actual remembered one, so visualisation is an incredibly powerful tool to help you create your future just the way you want it to be. One of the great ways in which to utilise this powerful tool is to create a vision board. You could use a notice board, a stiff piece of cardboard, or even a piece of paper (if that is all that you have handy) but start to collect pictures of things that you want to create in your life. Maybe it is your dream house. If so, cut out a picture of the house that you want to live in and stick or pin it on your vision board. If its prosperity that you want, write yourself a cheque for the amount that you would like and stick it on your vision board or pin up some pictures of cash. If it's a car you dream of, stick that there as well. Basically anything that you want or dream of creating in your life put a picture, photo or statement on your vision board. You could print and stick inspirational words if you wish, peace, love, happiness, in fact anything that makes you feel good and helps you achieve the vibrational frequency that will in turn help you create your dream reality.

Put your vision board in a place where you will see it often and add to it whenever you choose. Remember when looking at it you need to imagine how you will feel when you have the things you desire, whether it be peace, happiness, prosperity or physical items such as a house, car, weight loss, new clothes etc. Let yourself be inspired and believe that it is already yours. Be grateful for all of the good things already in your life and acknowledge The Law of Attraction in action.

I always look at my vision board first thing in the morning and last thing at night. Most of all, enjoy every moment of believing that all of your dreams ***can*** and ***will*** come true. You are the master of your reality and it starts right here, right now!

Create A Wish List

"You can have anything you want if you will give up the belief that you can't have it."

~Dr. Robert Anthony~

I would like to tell you about a positive surprising experience I had whilst I was sorting through a pile of old papers and letters that had been forgotten in the back of a cupboard.

Some years back, when I had only just learned about the Law of Attraction, I decided to write a wish list of all of the things that I wanted. Being new to this, my requests were fairly modest. I asked for a new lawn mower as mine had broken down, I wanted a new phone, better health as I was quite ill at the time, a holiday to Jamaica (I even specified the hotel), some new clothes for a certain event and many more things. I visualised them, thanked the Universe for them (as if they had already come to me) and then accidentally the list was swept into a pile with other papers, shoved into the back of the cupboard and forgotten about. At the time they were written, although modest requests, they were quite out of my reach financially.

When I rediscovered this old list I was absolutely amazed by the outcome of these requests. ***Every single one of them had come true!***

Within a few months of the requests I had received a new lawnmower through a recycle organisation and I didn't have to pay a penny! I was bought a new mobile phone as a gift and guess what? It was the exact model I wanted even though I hadn't told anyone. My health improved dramatically. Whilst searching for deals to Jamaica, the very hotel that I wanted was on special offer and I managed to afford it due to unexpected cash coming my way. My mum decided to treat me to new clothes even though I hadn't mentioned the event that I needed them for to her. Every single request had come true to my amazement and all of them within a few months of my list being written!

Sometimes it takes experiences like these to give us a kick. To remember how wonderful and bountiful the Universe really is and how powerfully The Law of Attraction plays a part in our lives.

Give it a go yourself. You have absolutely nothing to lose. Write it on a scrap of paper as I did or write it on a fancy piece of card and attach pictures of your requests alongside it to make it a part wish list - part vision board. It's up to you how you do it, but remember, follow it up with positive thought, vibrations, actions and belief. And then, just watch as the things you have asked for come true!

Take Care Of The Little Things -The Big Will Follow!

" If you can imagine it, you can create it. If you can dream it, you can become it."

~ William A Ward~

In the previous chapters I talked about how visualisation is a powerful tool. I had explained that it is sometimes difficult to believe that the larger things you may want could come true due to our own self limiting beliefs. The Universe does not distinguish between a small shack or a large mansion or £1 or £1,000,000. So an effective way to build up your confidence in the Law of Attraction is to start small. I am going to explain how I did it.

One of the easiest and quickest ways I found to build that confidence is manifesting something that you have lost. You know that feeling when you lose something? You have no idea where it is. Maybe you left it somewhere for 'safe keeping' and it was so safe you forgot where you put it! Well, just ask the Universe to guide you to the object. Briefly visualise the object and how it feels in your hands and then clear your mind. Don't over think it, just let your subconscious take you to search for it. When I do this, I always find what I am looking for within a few moments. It ***always*** works if you believe in it.

Another thing I do (I discovered this through the film and book 'The Secret') is to ask for a parking spot exactly where you want it to be. I know that most people have been frustrated by going to a location and have been unable to find a parking spot where they wanted it. Well I simply imagine in my mind where I want to park, I ask the Universe to make it available for me and I imagine myself parking there. ***Without fail*** I always find a space either on the exact spot or within a couple of cars to that spot. On the odd occasion I had to wait maximum of a minute or so for the spot, but I always get it.

You may have your own ideas about what it is you want to ask for. Go for it! Maybe its money that you need. Go ahead and ask for it, imagine how it looks in your hands as you count it or how it will look on a cheque or in your bank account, but whatever you do, don't ask with a feeling of lack because if you do you will be attracting exactly that, lack! Make sure that you always believe in your request. Feel the joy when visualising it as if you already own whatever it is you want, in fact, thank the Universe for bringing it to you. This is why I said start small and build up your belief until you know beyond any doubt that the Universal Law of Attraction exists and works for you!

One other thing. When you get your request, don't forget to show your gratitude and send out thanks as this will attract more and more positive things into your life.

The Danger Of Self Limiting Beliefs

"Out of our beliefs are born deeds; out of our deeds we form habits; out of our habits grows our character; and on our character we build our destiny." ~Henry Hancock~

Self limiting beliefs are very dangerous as they stop you reaching your full potential. You are the master of your own fate and you create your own reality. You need to seriously start to consider whatever it is that you are focusing on, because if it is negative, that is what you will be attracting back to you, negativity. And if you are a person who is looking for the positive in any situation, then you will in time better your situation because you will be attracting positive things.

A lot of people are unable to think in a positive way because from a very early age they have been instilled with negative thinking. They may have been taught to be cautious of money, that to want more money is being greedy, hence they believe deep down that money is bad. They may have been made to feel bad about their body size or shape by their peers or maybe their own parents! So naturally they have no self esteem and think that they are ugly or fat. Some people have parents who have always told them to 'err on the side of caution' and always see the cup as 'half empty' as opposed to 'half full', but whatever the self limiting beliefs that have been embedded in you as a child, you need to get rid of these as soon as possible because they will most definitely stop you from reaching your full potential. You may ask how I can do that? Well, affirmations are a tool that are very helpful in getting rid of self limiting thoughts, I cover this in the chapter about 'Building Confidence'. But you can start right here, right now, by monitoring your thoughts and beliefs.

Instead of thinking 'How can I possibly pay my bills? I have so little money.' Try to think instead 'Money is on the way to me right now, money is good, it will give me financial Independence.' Believe it as you say it and visualise how that money will feel in your hands, knowing that you can buy anything that you want and how wonderful it will be to debt free. Relish that feeling of freedom, let it wash over you and wipe out any resistance you may be holding. Believe me, if you change your thinking in this way the Law of Attraction will respond and in turn attract more money into your life.

How fast and how much money will correspond with how much you ask for and how strong your belief is. In the same way when thinking about your body shape/size, don't put yourself down. Instead believe that you are on the road to changing your body the way that you want to. Imagine yourself the way that you wish to be. If you have a photo of days when you were slimmer put that up on your vision board and look at it daily and believe that it is possible to look like that again. Throw away all of these self limiting beliefs and change the cycle. This can apply to any self limiting beliefs that you may have, whatever they are, whatever the subject.

Start thinking positive. Give thanks daily for all of the good things in your life and watch the changes that start to happen with joy and amazement and then... give thanks again!

The Law Of Attraction And Forgiveness.

"Focus on the best you can in others; and

when characteristics you want are missing,

practice seeing them anyway - for when you

practice the thoughts of the things that you desire,

they must show up in your experience."

~Abraham-Hicks~

Today I wanted to take the time to explain the importance of forgiveness. To forgive someone for something that they have done to you is a very powerful force and not just for them, it's for your benefit too!

Let me explain. You may know someone in your life who is bitter, maybe it's a work colleague, maybe a relative or friend or maybe it's you. Bitterness is an understandable thing but it is very damaging. I know women who have been treated very badly by boyfriend after boyfriend until they no longer believe that a happy healthy relationship is possible in their lives. They have become bitter about this until they no longer look at men or dates with a view to having a happy relationship, instead they expect the worse from the very beginning and are in fact looking for it.

You guessed it, the Law of Attraction gives them exactly what they are looking for. They are self perpetuating the cycle and time after time, relationship after relationship turns sour, because they have attracted it by expecting it.

This can apply to anything. You (or people that you know) may have suffered in any kind of way at the hands of other people or just difficult circumstances in your life. But holding on to it, mulling it over again and again in your mind is only hurting you. The Universe doesn't differentiate between a negative vibration or a positive vibration, it will only respond to what you are sending out and respond in kind with more of the same. So you can see the importance of rooting out all of those negative emotions that you may be clinging on too. No matter what someone has done to you it ***is*** possible to let go and move on. It may be difficult initially especially if we are talking about childhood hurts and memories, but to hold on to them is to be living the same bad memories on a daily basis. You may as well resign yourself to being the victim forever. Do you really want that?

"Forgiveness does not change the past, but it does enlarge the future."

~Paul Boese~

Being in the company of people who are always negative can also have a negative effect on you. To be around someone who is constantly moaning about debt or relationship issues or other negative things that they may be experiencing can be quite draining. Whilst your attention is focused on their problems you are also sending out the same negative vibe and attracting those negative things back into ***your*** life. It is a difficult situation to deal with because these people may be your friends or even close relatives and you obviously don't want to turn your back on them.

So what can you do? Well the obvious answer would be to share with them your knowledge of The Law of Attraction. Explain how it can change their life for the better. Try and get them to give thanks for all of the good things in their life. This is a positive way to help and uplift a person who is feeling down. To sit and agree with every negative thing that they are saying will not help them at all and will be in fact injuring yourself into the bargain. If someone persists in being negative even when you are trying to uplift them it would be well advised to try and distance yourself emotionally otherwise you will most definitely be dragged on the roller coaster of negative emotions that they themselves are going through. Offering solutions rather than focusing on the problem is also a positive way of helping others.

Remember, the Law of Attraction is obedient to your every wish. If you are focusing and wishing for good and happy things in your life - that is what you will receive! If you are focusing or remembering the negative, and mulling over all of the wrongs that have happened in your life, you will be sending out the signal that this is what you expect and so the Law of the Universe will oblige and send you more of the same.

You can change your life, right here, right now. Let go, forgive, and watch how the pattern will change and your life will become so enriched with joy and happiness that you will scarcely recognise the 'old you'!

'Allowing' Your Desires To Come True.

"If you will relax and allow Law of Attraction to do the organization, the managing, then you can spend your time doing the things that please you." ~Abraham Hicks~

In previous chapters I have talked about how to change your self-limiting beliefs in order to change your thoughts which in turn change the vibrations that you are sending out. But there is one more step in the process of attracting your dreams and desires and turning them into reality. It is called 'Allowing'.

It might sound really obvious, to 'allow' your requests to come true, but in fact it is a stumbling block for many people when they are trying to utilise The Law Of Attraction for positive changes in their lives. A lot of people fall at this final hurdle and then give up on the Law of Attraction believing it to not exist. The truth is that whether or not you believe in The Law Of Attraction, it is a fact of life in the same way that electricity or the Law of Gravity exists even though we cannot see it. The Law Of Attraction is always working in your life, it is changing and forming your reality ***right now*** with the very thoughts and emotions that are going through your mind. It is attracting more of the same whether or not they are positive thoughts and emotions or negative ones.

This is why it is so important to harness our thoughts and emotions to work for us, not against us!

Let me explain. So you have visualised what you want. You have sent out the right positive emotions and you are being very careful to be positive in your day to day life. But have you 'allowed'? Are you receiving what you have requested? If not, it could be because you haven't 'allowed' it.

What is 'allowing'? It is simply the absence of doubt and resistance. You have to remove any doubt and resistance from the process. Doubt is a negative emotion and straight away it will undo any good you may have been doing with your visualisations. The strong positive vibration you have been sending out is being cancelled out by the vibrations of doubt that you have been thinking. You have to fully believe that your requests will come true, no matter what. I know that this can be difficult to achieve which is why I wrote a previous chapter about how to 'Take Care Of The Little Things -The Big Will Follow!' It is far better to start by asking for small things that you believe are possible and build confidence in the process, than to always be asking for big things but not really believing that they are possible, because this will in turn make you doubt, remember, negative always attracts negative! So start 'allowing' today and watch how your dreams start to become your reality.

Telling A New Life Story

"Watch your thoughts, they become words. Watch your words, they become actions. Watch your actions, they become habits. Watch your habits, they become character. Watch your character, for it becomes your destiny." ~Upanishads~

Most of us at some point in our lives have been guilty of telling our life story and making it sound as if it is inevitable that difficult or bad things happened to us. I know I have! It would normally start by a friend asking about some aspect of my past and would end in me spouting out endless tales of woe and misery as I remembered and recounted each and every painful detail. I would feel the misery wash over me as I wailed 'Why did this have to happen to me?' Little did I know that each and every time I did this I was making sure that I was creating more tales of woe to tell for the future!

"If you examine your history, you cannot help but repeat it! Law of Attraction says it is so: 'Whatever I am looking at, I am including in my vibration.'" ~Abraham Hicks~

No one wants to live each day in misery. Yet we so often do, simply by remembering or talking about bad things that have happened to us. Sometimes there is almost a sick kind of pleasure by gossiping about how this happened and that happened, almost a kind of ***'but my life is harder than yours'*** mentality. But if I told you that by this very kind of talk you are bringing yourself more and more of the same kind of problems and misery, would you carry on doing it? Of course not.

Remember, the Law of Attraction ***always*** brings us what we think about and focus on. If we are thinking about and focusing on negative things, of course our vibration will also be negative and the Law of Attraction will oblige by bringing us more of those negative experiences. This is why you will always see one person who seems to be unlucky in love with a series of disastrous relationships or another may be always in debt and has money worries or maybe another person you know is always afflicted with ailments and illness. The chances are they are always talking about these negative experiences and mulling over them, believing that nothing will change and indeed, until they change their story - nothing ***will*** change!

True example: A friends 9 year old daughter was constantly bed wetting. The whole family obsessed about this bed wetting and would always be very negative when talking to the child about it. I would often hear comments like, 'I suppose there will be a wet bed to change tomorrow again!' or, 'Not wet again are you? When will you grow out of this!' and other comments of this nature. When they finally understood how the Law of Attraction works they started instead to make comments like 'I bet you are going to be dry this week aren't you?' and 'How wonderful it is now that she is dry'. They no longer talked and worried about it. They put it from their minds and if there was a wet bed to deal with it was done with the minimum of fuss and bother. Within a month this child was no longer wetting the bed. It simply stopped. Once the focus was off the negative and positive comments were made, the reality followed suit. They now use the Law of Attraction in all aspects of their life.

So starting today, change your story, start to ***tell it as you want it to be*** not the negative things it has been in the past. Every second of the day we are creating our immediate and long term future. But the good news is we can change how we tell our story immediately and then once we see the changes manifesting themselves in our lives it becomes no longer difficult to talk about our positive life story as we want it to be - because it will already be a reality!

How To Attract Money Into Your Life

"Prosperity is a way of living and thinking, and not just money or things. Poverty is a way of living and thinking, and not just a lack of money or things." ~Eric Lutterworth~

Money is a controversial subject and many people feel uncomfortable about asking the Universe for money as if it is somehow wrong and greedy to do so and yet all of us need money to live. We use it to pay our rent, to buy food, to pay for bills and to buy those things that make life enjoyable. Most people simply want to be debt free whilst others want full financial freedom, and this is how we should consider money, as freedom. Freedom from stress, freedom from debt and freedom from poverty.

There is nothing wrong in any way with wishing for enough money to gain our full financial freedom and Independence.

We were born to live a life of abundance. It is only our self limiting beliefs that hold us back from achieving this. By self limiting beliefs I mean to say that some of us have been brought up since birth to believe that to want money is greedy, bad and not right. Some people whilst wanting more money believe deep down that they don't deserve it and shouldn't really be yearning for it, but if they only examine their need for money closely, it isn't really money for moneys sake that they are wanting, it is financial independence, to be free from worry, to own their own house, to be able to buy what they want when they want it. There is absolutely nothing wrong with this. Abundance is our birth right. But their self limiting beliefs could well be holding them back in achieving their goals. The previous chapter on Self Limiting Beliefs talks about this in more detail.

Just the fact of needing money in itself will not attract it. In fact if you are constantly sending out vibrations of need that is exactly what you will attract back - need! You must change your old negative vibrations of need to positive vibrations of thankfulness for that what you currently have. Then using visualisation you need to imagine how wonderful you are going to feel as you buy that house of your dreams, as you pay off all of your bills, as you see cheques dropping on your door mat and as your bank account swells and you can buy whatever you want. You should feel these emotions as if it has already happened and give thanks to the universe for it as if you already have it. Do this daily, ***be specific*** in how much money you want, don't get hung up on how the money will come to you, just send out the request and then 'allow' it. Make sure that you believe in what you are asking for though, because if you send out signals of doubt it will cancel out all of your good work and slow or even halt your manifestation. Affirmations are a great tool to cancel out resistance.

"You are a creator; you create with your every thought. You often create by default, for you are getting what you are giving your attention to wanted or unwanted but you know by how it feels if what you are getting (creating) is what you are wanting or if it is not what you are wanting. (Where is your attention focused?)"

~Abraham Hicks~

Remember the Law of Attraction does not distinguish between £1 or £100,000 it is only your mind that does that, so really the sky is the limit as long as you believe in it. Obviously the money isn't going to fall out of the sky and land at your feet but you need not worry about how it will come about. The Universe will sort it out. It could come in the form of extra work, a change of career with much better pay, a gift or a win or any number of other ways. Be alert for opportunities that the universe will send your way. Things will suddenly start to happen that will turn your request into reality. All you have to do is visualise, remain positive in all aspects of your life, give daily gratitude for all the good in your life and continue to believe that this is your divine right to have abundance, joy, happiness, health and a future that you yourself have created. Don't forget to act on any inspired ideas or opportunities that come your way and then watch as your dreams, hopes and aspirations come true!

Here are a few examples of affirmations that target abundance and prosperity. It can be helpful to say these in the morning before you start your day, at night before bed or at any time when you feel doubt and resistance. With persistence, all doubt and resistance will fall away and be replaced with belief and joy as you watch your reality change before your eyes

- Prosperity overflows in my life. I have everything in abundance.
- Prosperity overflows in my life. I have everything in abundance.
- Money flows in my life in abundance.
- My thoughts are always about abundance and prosperity.
- All my actions lead to abundance and prosperity.
- I focus on abundance and prosperity and thereby attract it to me.

- Prosperity within me, prosperity around me; abundance within me, abundance around me.
- I let go of all resistance to prosperity and it comes to me naturally.
- The whole Universe and entire mankind is conspiring to make me prosperous and abundant.
- I love abundance and prosperity and I attract it naturally.
- I allow all good things to come into my life and I enjoy them.
- I create prosperity easily and effortlessly.
- Abundance and prosperity is my birthright and I have it.
- I am in a state of fulfilment, have abundant love and joy in my life and am free to do whatever I wish to do.
- I am prosperous, healthy, happy and live in abundance.
- I am thankful for the abundance and prosperity in my life.

Building Confidence Using The Law Of Attraction

"Never be bullied into silence. Never allow yourself to be made a victim. Accept no one's definition of your life; define yourself."

~Harvey Fienstein~

Self confidence is the key to success. Just about every life coach, psychologist and other professionals agree on this, but it is easier said than done.

Using the Law of Attraction properly it is possible to change the way that you feel about yourself and how others see you. I know that to someone who has suffered abuse and bullying at the hands of others this may be difficult to believe and some people will indeed need specialist help to get over their past. But there is one thing to remember, The Law of Attraction is shaping your life ***right now*** whether you know it or not. Therefore it is possible to start to change the way that you think about yourself and your life ***immediately***. Even if it is in small steps. The chapter on 'Telling a New Life Story' has more information on this. Forgiveness is also a powerful tool in which you can change your life and help you to believe in yourself, see the chapter about 'Forgiveness and the Law of Attraction'.

Affirmations can be a very strong tool to start with. Instead of having negative thoughts running inside your head you must nip them in the bud and change them. For example when you do something silly, don't castigate yourself over it. Don't think 'I am so stupid, I never do anything right' or 'Who would want me, I have nothing to offer'. You need to immediately catch that thought and change it to 'I do a lot of things that are right' and 'I have a lot to offer and am a wonderful person'. It might not be easy at first and it might not seem real, but if you stick at it, eventually you will train your mind to think much more positively and it will become natural to think that way. If you find this difficult to do, a good tip is to list and affirm all of the things you like about yourself, even if it's just one thing, focus on that.

Affirmations are a wonderful way to get into the practise of self belief. Some people say them each morning before they start their day and the last thing at night before bed, but you can say them at any time of the day or night and always use them when self doubt starts to creep back in. The following affirmations may be particularly helpful for self esteem and confidence issues:

- I have the right to happiness and abundance.
- I am worthy of all the good things that the Universe can offer me.
- I am successful in all my endeavours.
- I am flexible and open to change in all aspects of my life.
- I can make my own choices and decisions.
- I have the power to change myself and therefore my life story.
- I am beautiful inside and out.
- I deserve to be loved.
- I choose happiness whatever my circumstances.
- I am able to forgive others and understand their motives.

- I have forgiven myself for any past mistakes and I believe that to do my best is enough.
- My high self esteem allows me to accept compliments easily and also freely compliment others.
- I accept others as they are and they in turn accept me as I am.
- It matters little what others say. What matters is how I react and what I believe.
- I have high self esteem as I respect myself.
- I deserve all that is good. I release any need for misery and suffering.

Tip: If you are in a particularly negative mindset when you first start to use affirmations, they can feel like a lie. It can often help for the first few days to start the affirmation with 'I am in process of ...' i.e. the affirmation 'I am successful in all my endeavours' could be changed to 'I am in the process of being successful in all my endeavours' This can be more believable to you and therefore you will be sending out a believable strong positive vibration instead of a doubtful fearful one. Once you get comfortable saying it this way you should then move on to the full, powerful version as written above.

You can use any affirmations that suit you and your current situation, but remember they must always be positive. Some people find it helpful to say theirs in front of the mirror. Do whatever makes you comfortable. But the most important thing is to keep it up. Don't expect instant results though, it can take a while to change the negative thought processes of a lifetime. But if you are vigilant and stop the negative thought processes even as they enter your mind, ***you can and will*** stamp them out and replace them with positive and joyful thoughts. As you know, The Law of Attraction works like a magnet and will attract whatever vibrations you are sending out, so if they are negative vibrations then the things you will attract into your life will be negative, but if it is largely positive thoughts, emotions and vibrations that you are thinking and sending out, then you will be attracting positive things, emotions and people into your life.

Your life can change for the better ***right here right now***. Just make up your mind to do it and the sky is the limit!

Attracting Your Dream Partner

"Love is an energy: it can neither be created nor destroyed. It just is and always will be, giving meaning to life and direction to goodness."

~ Bryce Courtney~

The Law of Attraction is a marvellous thing. It can be used in many powerful ways to increase your happiness and change your life for the better. One of these ways is to attract your dream partner.

Most people talk about meeting their 'soul mate', their life partner. If you are looking for yours then you are very likely to know exactly what you ***don't want***, but do you really know what it is that you ***do want*** in a life partner?

Before the Universe can send you your heart's desire, you yourself have to first know what it is that you want in your life partner. Are you are constantly thinking and mulling over your past relationships and how those persons were wrong for you? Maybe they were unfaithful or not supportive or any other number of negative things. But remember, what you are thinking about and the emotions that accompany the thoughts will only bring you more of the same. Positive attracts positive, negative attracts negative. So you need to change that unhealthy cycle of attracting bad or unsuccessful relationships and start fresh, instead attracting what you do want.

A good exercise to understand what you do really want in a life partner is to make a list. Take a piece of paper and draw a vertical line right down the middle. Just this one time I need you to consider what you ***don't want*** in a partner. It wouldn't be wise to do this ***'don't want'*** list too regularly as it is could create resistance from unpleasant previous relationship memories, but it is important to this exercise to do it this once.

List all of the things you ***don't want*** on the left hand side then using this negative list as contrast make a list of the opposite attributes on the right hand side (the positive side), using what you don't want as a reference. For example: Unfaithful - Faithful or Unsupportive - Supportive, and so on, until you have your complete list. Once it is finished you can then re-write or print out the list of only the things that you ***do want*** in your new life partner (discarding the 'don't want' list). Be exact in what you would like, even down to shared hobbies if that is what you would like. You can then either pin this list wherever you like or add it to your vision board (please see the chapter on Vision Boards for more information).

When reviewing this new list of the attributes of your future life partner, thank the Universe for bringing him or her to you as if you are already together. Imagine how wonderful it will be when you are doing the things that you love together! Let your emotions free as you make this request, making sure that it is positive emotions you are sending out, not feelings of loneliness or lack.

The Law of Attraction will send to you exactly what you are thinking and feeling so make sure that you change your old pattern of thinking. Do not allow feelings of hurt, anger or bitterness from previous relationships cloud your mind, instead fill your mind with feelings of happiness, peace, contentment and love - just watch as the Universe brings you opportunities to meet the partner of your dreams.

Remember though, once you have your dream partner in your life, you need to continue to be and think positive and give thanks daily. This will strengthen your relationship. Then be amazed as your future unfolds in just the way you want it to.

How To Make Your Dreams Come True!

"Whatever you create in your life, you must first create in your imagination."

~Tycho Photiou~

What is it that ***you*** dream about? Do you even know what it is that you really want right now? What are your life goals? When you know the answers to these questions then you are half way there to manifesting them.

Sometimes we get so bogged down with the mundane struggles of life, paying the bills, fixing the car or looking after our kids, that we sometimes forget the wider picture. Surely as a young teenager you didn't think 'Wow! I can't wait to grow up so I can worry about bills and kids and keeping my car on the road!'

Of course you didn't. Most of us had bigger dreams and goals. Maybe some of them came true and maybe a whole lot of them fell by the wayside. Maybe your dreams changed as you got older. Either way, I am here to let you know that you really can manifest your dreams into reality. ***Its within your power to do so.***

The first step though is to know what it is that you truly want ***right now***. I know that you wouldn't go to the supermarket and buy fish if you don't even like fish and you wouldn't go and buy meat if you were vegetarian. You are very clear about your tastes in food and you need to be that specific about the rest of your dreams and desires. Take time out when you know that the house is quiet and put pen to paper. Write out some lists. Start with a 'Life Goal' list. List every life goal that you want to accomplish, don't feel shy, think big! If you want to be a successful business person, write it down. If you want to be a doctor or a lawyer, write it down. If you want to be a artist, a job that takes you around the world or simply be a person who is able to help others, write it down. List it clearly. If you have more than one thing that you want to accomplish write them down, The Universe is bountiful it is not going to say 'you have to choose only one!'

Then you can move on to a relationship list, a financial list, a material possession list and so on. Be specific. Sometimes it may require that you acknowledge what it is that you ***don't*** want in order to see what it is that you really ***do*** want. This is called ***contrast***.

Once these are done, you can then do the fun part. Every day, as many times as you like, visualise something on your list coming true. Taste it. See it. Feel it. Enjoy it. Send thanks out into the Universe as if it has already come true. Most of all, believe it and allow it. Then one day in the future take a real good look at your lists and be amazed as you start to realise that The Law of Attraction really works and your dreams are now your reality.

"I am no longer cursed by poverty because I took possession of my own mind, and that mind has yielded me every material thing I want, and much more than I need. But this power of mind is a universal one, available to the humblest person as it is to the greatest."

~Andrew Carnegie~

Recognising Sent Opportunities

"Action that is inspired from aligned thought is joyful action. Action that is offered from a place of contradicted thought is hard work that is not satisfying and does not yield good results. When you really feel like jumping into action, that is a clear sign that your vibration is pure and you are not offering contradicting thoughts to your own desire. When you are having a hard time making yourself do something, or when the action you offer does not produce the results you are seeking, it is always because you are offering thoughts in opposition to your desire."

~Abraham Hicks~

Have you been applying The Law of Attraction in your life? Making your wish list, your dream board, visualising daily and then wondering why the things that you want are not manifesting in your life?

It could be that the Universe is sending you the answers but that ***you*** are not recognising them!

The Universe doesn't conjure up items, money and the people that we wish to attract by magic. What actually happens is that once you have understood what it is that you want in your life, visualised it daily, given thanks as if it is already here and believed that it will come you, the Universe starts things rolling. It puts things in motion that will lead to you getting your heart's desire but you will still have a part to play. To explain this I would like to repeat an old story that you may have already heard.

There is a major storm coming to a town, and the residents are advised to evacuate. A car drive's by a neighbour's house, and the driver yells out to the neighbour. 'Do you need a ride?' The man declines, saying, 'God will save me.'

The rain becomes fierce, and now the town is flooded. A neighbour paddles by in a boat. He asks the man if he wants to get onboard. The man answers, 'No, God will save me.'

The man's house becomes so flooded, that he seeks safety up on his roof. A helicopter flies by, with the pilot yelling out, 'We'll lower our ladder so you can get on the copter.' Again, the man declines.

Eventually, the man drowns, and goes before God. The man angrily asks God why He let him die. 'I've always been a righteous man. I never missed church. Why didn't you save me?'

God answered, 'I sent you a man in a car, and a man in a boat, and a man in a helicopter.'

The moral of the story being that we could be staring at the answers to our wishes right in the face and not be able to recognise them. I would like to tell you a true story of a businessman I know of. He had been asking the Universe to send him more money. He wanted to buy a bigger house for his family, be able to afford to decorate and furnish it and then take his family on a long holiday as one of his sons had just recovered from Leukaemia.

He asked, he made a vision board, he visualised and he knew it would come true (after all other things he had asked for had come to him in the past) but as he waited and waited and waited he started to question the power of the Universe because he wasn't seeing cheques landing on his doorstep, he wasn't seeing people queuing up at the door to give him contracts and he started to doubt. Meanwhile a scruffily dressed man had been asking to see him every day with a crackpot idea for an invention. It was something seemingly stupid, that could never work, so after hearing about it briefly as he entered the office one day he thereafter ignored the man and instructed his secretary to not let him into the office.

Day after day when he entered the office he saw the man sitting outside always pleading with him to give him a few minutes to talk about his invention. After this had been going on for a few weeks, annoyed, he finally decided to give the man five minutes just to get rid of him!

The man launched into his spiel about his invention enthusiastically talking about how and where it could be sold. The businessman suddenly sat up and took notice. Not of the product that the man had invented, but of the technology behind it! When he questioned the man he found out that the man had patented the technology so it was legally his to do as he pleased with. To cut a long story short. They both ended up making millions and the businessman learned a valuable lesson.

One of the most important thing about The Law of the Attraction is not to pre-judge how your wish may come true but to allow the Universe to do its work, be vigilant and to explore carefully any opportunity that may come your way as it may be the answer that you have been looking for. Sometimes it may be easy and could come in the form of more work, a better job or even cheques landing on the doorstep but sometimes it could need a little more diligence on your part.

The same principle applies when looking for that perfect life partner, career or anything on your wish list. Don't try and tell the Universe how you want it to come about. Just put your wish out there, follow the basic principles of the Law of Attraction: positivity, visualisation and belief (allowing). Then watch as the Universe will set into motion the means and ways for your dreams to become reality.

Feelings Are The Key!

"Happiness is not a destination. It is a method of life." ~ Burton Hills~

This point was covered briefly in another chapter but it is such a important point I felt it deserved a chapter of its own.

Visualisation, Dream Boards and Affirmations all have their place in assisting us to change our thought process to one of abundance and happiness and when we are sending out these positive vibrations to the Universe, this in turn then attracts those things that we want into our lives. But how do you know if you are on the right track?

The key to knowing you are in the process of receiving that which you want into your life is how you are ***feeling.*** If you are feeling bad, sad, depressed, low, angry, jealous or any of the other negative emotions that we all feel time to time, just know that you have put a halt or are slowing down the process of you getting that which you wish for. Whether that is wealth, health, happiness, meeting the ideal partner or any other wishes you may have, the negative emotions you are feeling are slowing down the process and could in fact be attracting that which you ***don't*** wish for into your life!

The good news is that this can be reversed very easily. If you know what it is making you feel bad then simply change it! I know this sounds easier said than done, but it is very simple, if something or someone is making you feel bad then walk away from that situation. Obviously, if it is a friend or relative that is making you feel bad, it is easier said than done to remove them from your life especially if it is a person who is physically or otherwise dependant on you. But what ***is*** possible is how you react to that persons negativity and how often you spend time with them. Maybe you could try to educate them about the Law of Attraction and they can shift their point of attraction to a more positive vibe or maybe it is about how you manage your own emotions when around them.

In the short term if someone whom you cannot immediately write out of your life experience is affecting your vibration it can help to simply leave their presence when they are being particularly negative, go into a different room, do something that makes you feel better, read a book, listen to some uplifting music, play with a pet, whatever it is that makes you feel good will immediately shift your point of attraction to a positive one and thereby attract positive things into your life. In the long term, if you are practising ***feeling*** good then strange as it sounds you may find that negative people and situations automatically leave your life or they themselves will change their vibration and no longer be affecting your life experience negatively.

But what if I don't know *why* I am feeling bad?

It can be very difficult to always pinpoint what it is exactly that is making us feel bad and you may think that could be an obstacle to changing the way that you are feeling. But again there is good news, it doesn't really matter what it is making us feel bad, simply change that emotion by thinking of something that make you feel happy, go for a walk, put that uplifting music on, reminisce about something that makes you feel great (a birth or wedding or holiday etc) it doesn't matter what you think about or do - as long as you are feeling good!

Be secure in the knowledge that it is the way that you are ***feeling*** that will determine if your Visualisations, Wish list or requests to the Universe are coming true! By changing that emotion you are ***literally*** creating your reality, all the things that are negative in your life will change to positive things automatically, good things will start to happen to you, how strong your belief is in this and how often you feel positive emotions (Gratitude, Happiness, love, joy, contentment, abundance etc) will have an impact on how quickly you will see results. But be assured, if you are ***feeling*** good then good things are on the way!

It's All About The Journey

"I am not happy because of some extraneous circumstance. I am happy because I choose to be." ~Morris E. Wray~

All of the tools and exercises in this book are aimed at helping you create the life you have always dreamed about but at the end of the day it's all about the journey. It's human nature and its perfectly fine to have constantly changing goals and dreams. You will never get ***everything*** done as your goal posts will always be changing. This is the way it is meant to be, which is why enjoying every moment of your journey through life is so important. Once you are able to relax and enjoy the unfolding of each and every day, you will know that you have eliminated resistance and are in the process of 'allowing' . It shouldn't feel hard or a struggle, it should feel natural and right.

'Follow your bliss!' ~Abraham Hicks~

As long as you are enjoying your life its guaranteed that the things you want will come into your experience. Your inner guidance system...your emotions... will tell you everything you need to know about whether you are on the right path.

I wish you peace ,love and happiness and truly hope that this book has assisted you in your wonderful journey through life.

"Not what we have,

but what we enjoy,

constitutes our abundance."

~Epicurus quotes~

Dear Reader,

Thank you for buying this book. I truly hope it has made a difference in your life and wish you all the best in creating your own reality.

If you would like to connect further and be the first to hear about any up and coming books, please connect at:

https://www.facebook.com/shapereality/ or

https://createyourrealitytoday.blogspot.co.uk/

I would also welcome any feedback or comments.

Kind Regards

Nikki Roberts

27392857R00047

Printed in Great Britain
by Amazon